For my sister, Erica, whose strength and courage
are an inspiration
M.K.

Text copyright © 2014 by Monica Kulling
Illustrations copyright © 2014 by David Parkins

Published in Canada by Tundra Books,
a division of Random House of Canada Limited,
One Toronto Street, Suite 300, Toronto, Ontario M5C 2V6

Published in the United States by Tundra Books of Northern New York,
P.O. Box 1030, Plattsburgh, New York 12901

Library of Congress Control Number: 2013943889

Library and Archives Canada Cataloguing in Publication

Kulling, Monica, 1952-, author
      Spic-and-span! : Lillian Gilbreth's wonder kitchen / Monica Kulling ; illustrated by David Parkins.

(Great idea series)
Includes bibliographical references.
Issued in print and electronic formats.
ISBN 978-1-77049-380-3 (bound). – ISBN 978-1-77049-381-0 (epub)

      1. Gilbreth, Lillian Moller, 1878-1972 – Juvenile literature.
2. Women industrial engineers – United States – Biography – Juvenile literature. I. Parkins, David, illustrator II. Title. III. Series: Great idea series

T55.85.G84K84 2013   j658.5'4092   C2013-904500-7
                                                 C2013-904501-5

Sources of inspiration:

Gilbreth, Jr., Frank B. and Ernestine Gilbreth Carey. *Cheaper by the Dozen.* New York: Harper Perennial, 2002.

Graham, Laurel. *Managing on Her Own: Dr. Lillian Gilbreth and Women's Work in the Interwar Era.* Norcross, Georgia: Engineering & Management Press, 1998.

Lancaster, Jane. *Making Time: Lillian Moller Gilbreth – A Life Beyond "Cheaper by the Dozen."* Northeastern University Press, 2004.

http://www.engineergirl.org/CMS/WomenEngineers/Features/11783/11843.aspx.

Edited by Sue Tate

Designed by Leah Springate

The artwork in this book was rendered in pen and ink with watercolor on paper.

www.tundrabooks.com

Printed and bound in China

1 2 3 4 5 6   19 18 17 16 15 14

Lillian's Time
for Bobbi Miller

At the crack of dawn
as the sun spills orange
like the soft yolk oozing
from a well-timed egg

Lillian drinks a soothing tea
in the wicker by the window.
The day is not yet alive.
The house is not yet awake.

Lillian sips and thinks about
what she must do today
before her army of children
invades the quiet of her time.

Lillian and Frank Gilbreth lived in a large house in Montclair, New Jersey, with their eleven children. Every Sunday, the family loaded up the car and went for a drive.

Frank loved to blast the electric horn: *"Ahooga!"*

People stopped and stared. *Eleven children? Imagine!*

"Not too much horn," Lillian would say. She was a shy woman.

Lillian Moller Gilbreth was born in 1878 in Oakland, California. Her wealthy family had a mansion and servants, but Lillian did not want a pampered life. Unlike most girls of her time, she decided to go to university. Lillian wanted a life of adventure and challenge. When she married Frank Gilbreth in 1904, that's exactly what she got.

Lillian and Frank were "efficiency experts." They showed factory workers how to get the most done in the least amount of time. Frank thought there was one best way to do every job. Lillian thought people did their best when their workplace was comfortable and they enjoyed what they were doing. Lillian was not only an industrial engineer, but a psychologist too.

The Gilbreths used a new invention – the motion picture camera – to film a worker on the job. Then they studied the film to see if the worker was making unnecessary movements. They discovered that cutting out wasteful actions was the way to get more done and be less tired.

Lillian and Frank were efficient at home as well, running their house on the "Gilbreth System." Charts listed each child's "work": brushing their teeth, taking a bath, or making a bed. When the children completed a task, they placed a tick mark on the chart.

Once a week, the Gilbreths held family meetings. At one meeting, William piped up, "I want a dog."

"Never!" shouted Frank. "Dogs are messy."

"But," Lillian said calmly, "it would be good for the children to take care of an animal. And think of those happiness minutes."

The family voted. Frank lost. Soon there was a dog at 68 Eagle Rock Way.

By 1924, Lillian and Frank's business, Gilbreth Inc., was famous in the motion-studies field. Frank was invited to give a speech at a conference in Europe. While he was at the train station picking up his ticket, he phoned Lillian to check on his passport. She put the phone down and went to find it.

When Lillian returned, there was no one on the line. Frank had collapsed in the telephone booth at the Lackawanna Train Station. He'd died of a heart attack.

Lillian now faced a mountain of worry. How would she bring up eleven children on her own? How could she earn enough money to pay for their food, clothing, and education?

Relatives offered to take in one child, maybe two. Lillian's mother offered her home to the entire family, so Lillian called a family meeting. "Shall we live in California with Grandma?" she asked.

The votes came in. *No!* They would all stay together in the big house in Montclair, New Jersey.

A few days after Frank's funeral, Lillian was on a ship bound for Europe. She'd decided to give Frank's speech at the conference so their work in the motion-studies field would not be forgotten.

When she returned, Lillian faced another problem: the Gilbreths needed money. Lillian sold the car and let the cook go. It was time that Lillian and her two older daughters, Ernestine and Martha, learned how to cook.

Lillian needed work, but the factories wouldn't hire a female industrial engineer. Even one with twenty years' experience!

Every day, William met Lillian at the door and asked, "Did you find a job yet, Mother?"

One happy day, Lillian replied, "Yes, I did."

Macy's, the biggest department store in the country, had hired Lillian to improve its cash-room operations.

In the 1920s, most stores did not keep money in cash registers. They used a compressed air chute system to collect the money in one place. The money was put into containers and shot – like spitballs through a straw – through the air chute to the cash room upstairs.

Right away, Lillian saw that Macy's cash room was noisy and poorly lit. The clerks were sitting on uncomfortable chairs. Soon Lillian turned all that around, and Macy's was a happy client.

At home, Lillian, Ernestine, and Martha were cooking up a storm. Dashing to and fro, they kept getting in each other's way.

Suddenly, Lillian scraped her fingers on a grater. *"Ow!"* she cried. Looking around her old-fashioned kitchen, she mused: *The kitchen is the heart of the home. It should run like clockwork.* She decided to bring her space-saving, step-saving ideas from the factory into her own home.

Lillian cut open a brown paper bag and sketched a layout for a kitchen that would be both practical and efficient.

Lillian's kitchen design was the first to use the circular approach to arranging work surfaces, appliances, and sinks. She made sure that the appliances were steps from each other and that the cupboards were easy to reach. Working in a kitchen was less tiring if everything was close at hand. It was 1927. Lillian Gilbreth had reinvented herself.

Soon the Brooklyn Borough Gas Company hired her to improve kitchen designs. Lillian was ready. She interviewed over four thousand women to find out what didn't work in their kitchens. Armed with that information, she designed kitchens that were organized, efficient, and comfortable to work in.

One day, Lillian and Martha were in the kitchen making Frank's beloved apple cake. Martha was beating the batter by hand. "This work is so tiring, Mother," she said.

Lillian stopped to think. *Why can't beaters do their work on their own?* She got busy designing an electric mixer. No more aching arms!

L illian began to wonder about other inefficient kitchen items, for example, the garbage can. *It would be so much easier if you didn't have to bend to lift the lid*, she thought. So Lillian invented a garbage can with a lid that opened when you stepped on the foot pedal.

Next came the refrigerator. Lillian invented the
compartments in the door to store things like butter,
eggs, and cheese.

Lillian even designed a desk for the homemaker to sit at while making up her weekly schedules and paying her bills. This innovation, called the Gilbreth Management Desk, was exhibited at A Century of Progress International Exposition in Chicago in 1933.

Lillian Gilbreth was a pioneer in "ergonomics" – the study of workplace design. Her ergonomic approach to kitchen design always kept the worker in mind.